A Scripture of Crows

Books by Charles Goodrich

POETRY

Insects of South Corvallis (2003)
Going to Seed: Dispatches from the Garden (2010)

PROSE

The Practice of Home (2004)
In the Blast Zone: Catastrophe and Renewal on Mount St. Helens
[co-editor] (2008)

A Scripture of Crows

Charles Goodrich

Silverfish Review Press
Eugene, Oregon

Cover art: Morris Graves, *Bird Experiencing Light*, 1969, Tempera on paper, 12-15/16 x 10-1/4 in. (32.9 x 26 cm), Seattle Art Museum, Eugene Fuller Memorial Collection 70.16.

Published by	Distributed by
Silverfish Review Press	Small Press Distribution
PO Box 3541	800-869-7553
Eugene, OR 97403	spd@spdbooks.org
www.silverfishreviewpress.com	www.spdbooks.org

ISBN 978-1-87885-163-5

Library of Congress Control Number: 2013906801

10 9 8 7 6 5 4 3 2 First Printing
Printed in the United States of America

Contents

III.

IV.

for Kapa and Elliot
and all the creatures of the home place

In the first of the moon,
All's a scattering,
A shining.

—Theodore Roethke

If it's darkness
we're having, let it be extravagant.

—Jane Kenyon

I.

Origins

Sitting on the porch with Ralph,
watching the lightning
riddle the sky
over the Seven Devils—

"That theory
where life started up
from lightning striking some soupy water—
that's just hooey.

Life had to have started up
on a morning like tomorrow's going to be,
the air scrubbed clean and all quiet

until some little clod of dirt
starts chirping for joy."

Burdock

Few seeds as tenacious as burdock,
clutching the dog's fur
tight as ticks. Burdock leaves
aren't as plush as mullein,
but they'll pass for kleenex in a pinch.

We haven't tried digging it up,
roasting the roots in an open pit,
then grinding them together with berries and fat
for pemmican yet,

but I own a sharp spade.
I'm not afraid to eat
woody things or bitter things,
or creatures that wiggle or squeal.

When I pull the burrs out of her fur,
the dog eats them.

Good dog.

A Distant Relative

A tiny leather pouch
with legs

and a wicked assortment of surgical tools in its mouth:
it's a tick
clinging to my sock,

a simple, blood sucking
bag of appetite,
and a generous purveyor of
Rocky Mountain spotted fever and Lyme disease. Its face
looks rather like a hole saw.

We are distantly related, I suppose,
if you go back far enough, back
to some inconceivably remote common ancestor,

like, say, my great-aunt Aggie's
great-great-uncle,
the family's legendary
parasite, who came home from Chancellorsville
toothless, emaciated, one-eyed, and crazy,
and built himself a tiny cabin at the back of the farm.

He wouldn't help
with the field work after the war, the story goes,
just wandered the pastures all day
chanting poems to the sheep

and like this tick
he died young
and none of his poems survive.

Touched

He complains that his shoulder blades ache
if there aren't any geese by the river
where the geese should be.

All summer he roams
the leftover woods, his hands
achy and cramped. He claims
that clawing huckleberries into his mouth
loosens the pain of the absence of bear.

I've seen him batting his eyes like crazy
in a garden without butterflies,
and sometimes his lips start twitching
as if he's trying to whistle a precise trill,
but even he can't tell what songbird it is
that no longer visits our town.

The last time we took him swimming
he stayed in the snowmelt river
turning redder and redder,
diving under again and again
to kick at the cobbles in the stream bed
until his feet were cut and bruised.

We all knew what wasn't there—
Chinook—but when we got him into the car
he said his eyelids wouldn't work
and for three terrible weeks
he couldn't close his eyes.

Morning Song at Billy Meadows

1

I can tell
the deer have been here
by the outward flow of the air.

2

The overnight rain has moved
into the ground, where it continues raining,
wending its way past worms.

3

The roots of the grasses are proud.
They think the rain has come to anoint them.
Grasses suffer the vanity of being plain.

4

Some flowers will die today
into seeds. My life
has pockets I've never emptied.

5

But the house cricket
will leave the house, and the field cricket
will come indoors.

6

And sometimes you realize
that the blood you gave to mosquito
is what makes the bluebird
so blue.

Government Work

Call it working-class
        Craftsman-style

this Forest Service cabin
        the CCC built in 1937
                beside Billy Meadows
                        in the conifer forest
in far northeastern Oregon.

The hand-built
        double plank front door
                has hand-forged hinges
the shape of tall pines.

The living room with its
        fir floors, pine paneling
                and a ceiling of clear pine boards
is like being inside a tree.

They used local basalt
        for the massive stone fireplace.
                The pine slab mantle
is black with their smoke.

Call it government work

all the trees felled and milled
        right here, everything built in place
                by young indigents learning a trade
as the world convulsed toward war.

Grinding Wheel

Back then
everything depended on blades—
on axes and pulaskis,
chisels and adzes, knives
in the kitchen, the tool shed, the barn,
a knife in every man's pocket.

That's why
the big grindstone—mounted
on a steel frame with a metal seat
and a foot treadle on the left side—still spins
on its well-greased bearing
implacable as a small planet.

They say
some old-timers
could whet a blade so fine
it would slide between the atoms
of wood or flesh, not cutting, not
drawing blood, just
probing the void.

Or maybe
that's only a story,
not what the grindstone is saying
in its gruff voice,
as I pump the treadle
and press my puny blade
to the wheel.

Wallowa County Weather

Sometimes a mess of clouds
will be heading this way,
I'll roll up the truck windows,
pour myself a cup of old coffee and go
sit on the front porch
waiting for the fireworks—

and nothing.
Maybe five drops of rain.

Just look at those fluffy clouds
out over Hells Canyon
starting to crowd one another and get
flat and black on the bottom.

Could be a gully washer coming,
or it could get clear as a window by sundown
and rain
nothing but stars.

Un-making the Sky

Our sky's blue
was an afterthought
of the flowers and trees
respiring oxygen into the atmosphere.

That brought improbable insects along
to shuttle their pollen.
And once there were bugs to eat
birds became thinkable.

Everyone who was paying attention
knew humans would be along soon
but no one imagined the sky
would go gray.

The Nature of Fear

You ask
if I was ever afraid up there,
alone for weeks and so far
from anybody.

A few times, yes.
Mostly I was studying
joy, reading and writing
in the company of mosquitoes
and quiet pine trees.

But once, out hiking,
I heard a dry branch snap close by,
then a chuffing grunt, and the sudden thought
bear
set my blood pumping.

And one night
I was startled awake—coyotes howling
mighty close—
though after my heart calmed I realized
what a fine trick that was.

The only time
I was dead frightened—
crazy, in fact, I wished I'd had a gun—
was when I woke up at something like 3 a.m. and heard
coming slow down the gravel road
a car.

II.

Filament

Last night
I heard the light bulb
above the kitchen sink
singing

its filament getting
thin
and rattling
with old age

And sure enough
this morning
it's burnt out
just like my mother

who gave off light
all those years
but only began to sing
toward the end

White Galaxy

My father would have been
a hundred years old today
though he died—gasping and
tugging at his landlady's bathrobe,
she told us at his funeral,
trying to stop her from calling an ambulance—well short
of seventy.

He published one novel
to good reviews on the advent
of the Great Depression
a couple of decades before I was born,
then quit writing to devote himself
to whiskey, and later,
gin.

We rarely saw each other
after my mother kicked him out, though I spent
the summer I was seventeen
living with him in Fresno.

I got a bad job
in a jam factory, and he bought me
a white Galaxy convertible
with red vinyl seats and a
failing transmission.

On the evenings we didn't go
to his AA meetings,
I would drive out to the reservoir
with a six-pack of Oly, park on the shoulder
and drink them one after another,

diligently, before they could lose
their chill,

engine ticking,
a few pale stars trying to penetrate
the Central Valley haze.

December 6, 2011

Flowers and Whistling

*"The Yana, although not approving of the occasional habit of dead souls to
return to the land of the living, accepted with considerable equanimity the fact
that they sometimes did so. They were said to visit places dear to them in life,
and flowers and whistling might attract them."*
—Theodora Kroeber, *Ishi in Two Worlds*

A cloud passes in front of the sun
and the sunflowers hang their heads.

A little wind pushes through the corn.
The green stalks clack together, then stand very still.

The last notes of my song
seep into the ground

and my old friend who has just gone
is the fragrance of the rose.

A Shrine

six cords of oak
every stick cut
exactly sixteen inches
then split and stacked
in long straight ricks

the man's strict love
of the physical world
inhabits this wood
and six years after his death
it still hurts to burn it

Black Bug

Hunched over the wheel
of his thirty-five-year-old Volkswagen,
snap-brim cap tugged low,
my old friend Richard
drives past the Courthouse
with two bales of straw wedged in the back seat.

He doesn't see me wave,
intent as he is on driving
well below the speed limit,
with a log truck bearing down on his tail,
downshifting,
blatting out black exhaust.

I can taste that trucker's anger,
the whole culture's impatience
with the Richards of the world
poking along, attending
to small things.

Among the few
who remain unseduced
by the glamour of speed, Richard
ages uncomplainingly, a John Keats
growing more peculiar by the day,
negative capability incarnate.

Fern in the Bumper

Bedridden, eyesight shot,
he couldn't work in the garden any more
or read. His fruit trees
hadn't been pruned for years
and his dahlias, undivided, grew
rank and mildewed.

When I stopped by
a few days before he died, the tires
of his old black Volkswagen
were nearly flat
and a sword fern had taken root in the back bumper.

So I won't mourn his death
exactly, only feel myself drawn
down murky inward paths, Richard leading me
around his vast garden, murmuring snatches of old poems
and making vague beckoning gestures
with arms like smoke.

At Rattlesnake Pass

All the way up Rattlesnake Grade,
as the van crawled around hairpin turns,
you told us about infamous wrecks,
the high-school friends you'd raced to Lewiston
just for kicks, one dead, another in a wheelchair.
"Stupid," you muttered, "just stupid kid stuff."

At the pass, we looked back down
at the winding switchbacks, the road
blasted into the steep juniper slopes,
the steel guard rail punched out in places.
You had a writer's enigmatic smile on,
a private story going in your mind.

When I asked why you were joining
the Marine Corps, you stared out the window
down at the creek in the depths of the canyon,
and said, finally, "I want to fly," then looked
right at me and added, "I need to live more
before I write."

Don't we all, I thought, as the van rolled
over the pass and we started down the Buford Grade.

Daoist Out of Kansas

"Because it was good, we were afraid." —William Stafford

Whatever happened to that guy from Kansas,
that fellow who talked to the grass? Remember him?
The one we'd find leaning to listen
underneath. Or we'd see him scanning the horizon
in the dark. He sure could breathe far.
Had a pet wind in his ear.

Remember when he tried to teach us the flat dance—
plain standing. And that song
for going along your own way called
grammar. Those little handsprings
he wrote every morning helped him master
himself, he said. Nobody else
had the patience, ornery as he was.

Maybe he's really gone or maybe
something else. I keep looking underneath
and listening far. He left us just enough.
Wish he could show us that cave once more, though,
and that great fear.

The Piano Tuner

With her head under the lid
of my hopeless spinet,
her voice comes out
minor-chorded—*I am sick
of tuning pianos. I need travel.
I need romance!*

Now she rifles through her toolbox
for a chisel, and she jabs it
toward my chest, *Don't you ever
waste a minute*, bones clicking
in her slender wrists. She's angry,
but more important she's

fifty
and broke
and her recently electric
love life's fizzling. On her knees
oiling the pedals, *I need to do something
hard*, her imperious
soul talking, spurring on
the slim, bursitic girl.

Too poor
to revisit Greece,
she's been talking with the Peace Corps
about Albania. *If I wanted a serious challenge
I'd go home to Raleigh
and take care of my parents.*

Dashing off a few quick scales, *That's it!*
That's all I can do. This piano
should be taken outside
and shot. With a cackling laugh
she bends to the keyboard, dark hair
falling over her face, and bangs out
a dirge.

I dreamed last night
I was on the beach
with a chain-smoking Greek.
He played the bouzouki
and I danced with the edge of the surf.

Rocks for Seeds

Thanks for sending me
this slab of siltstone
with the fossilized cone of *Metasequoia glyptostroboides*,
a dark thumbprint of mineralized lignin,
embedded in it,

evidence
that ten million years ago
a forest of Dawn Redwoods grew
in northeastern California
where now you raise sheep
at the edge of the Black Rock Desert.

For centuries
people thought Dawn Redwood
was extinct. Then a grove was rediscovered
on the grounds of a temple in Szechwan province
in 1944. From there its seeds
were disseminated
around the world.

I'm sending you these cones
from a tree growing beside the Music Building
at Oregon State University
in the hopes that swapping rocks for seeds
is a way to stay sane
on a planet where forests and deserts
routinely trade places.

Open the package gently.
The ripe seeds will have fallen
out of their cones. They'll be loose in the box.
They are hardly bigger
than grains of salt.

On the Day Clem Starck Goes in for Umbilical Hernia Surgery I Spade the Flower Beds under the Akebono Cherry Trees at the County Courthouse

No more carpentering for a while, Mr. Starck.
The surgeon prognosticates
a month-long recuperation.

Before you go under
tell the anesthesiologist
you want to wake up
here with me, under these heavenly
cherry blossoms.

And look at the worms, Clem!
Fertilizing with chicken manure
is the trick.

Remember the doctor says no lifting . . .
except books. I confess a pang
of envy: I'll be here on my knees, transplanting
salpiglossis,
while you're still in bed
reading everything
Basil Bunting ever wrote!

Camped in the Olympics

It's disturbing to crawl out
from a flimsy tent pitched far
up the Elwha and hear
this wild
laughing everywhere.

The stars
are rising like bubbles
in dark ale.
My companions are lost
in sleep. I crawled out here

to steady my dreams
with some cold sky.
Instead, hilarious
silence, the black trees
straining at the moon.

It's possible
I've never been so wholly
awake, but that laughing
isn't me, it isn't wolves,
and it isn't loons.

III.

The Uber-Rich Step Up

Mayor Bloomberg has vowed
to take shorter showers. The Koch brothers
are lowering the thermostat two degrees
in every one of their mansions. Rupert Murdoch
has ordered a fleet of Priuses
for his domestic staff.

When all the billionaires
of the Walton family changed to compact
fluorescent light bulbs, they saved enough energy
to buy Corpus Christi, Texas.

Corporations are doing their part, too:
Goldman Sachs is making compost
with five years of shredded account sheets,
while British Petroleum is recycling
advertising strategies from the tobacco industry.
Whole mountains are being removed
in the effort to bring you clean coal.

Change is in the air. Citizens,
we invite you to sit back
and watch it all happen on television.

Sleet Storm on Leap Day

February 29, 2012

Due to slippery streets,
the widespread anxiety
over just opened plum blossoms,

and the plunging barometer
of civility
in political discourse,

the regular Leap Day meeting of the Weird
Weather Worriers Club
has been rescheduled for February 29,
2016.

As always, we'll begin by singing the Wobbling
Planet Anthem and conclude
with the secret, sacred hand-
wringing.

Please be prompt.

Commonist

Gazing out the airplane window
at the intricately quilted
Sacramento River delta—

textured fields in tender hues of green,
white barns and black roads,
the channeled river and meandering canals—

I look back inside the plane to find
my fellow passengers
watching the in-flight movie.

Citizens! Let us now
look below
at our beloved country, our beautiful

and plundered landscape
and sing together in rude harmony
Woody Guthrie.

Ghost River

I thought I heard them again last night
hammering the Willamette,
walling it in and hooking up wires
as if the river were made of plastic and iron.

Through the fog of my dream
came an old steamboat
dredging the floodplain for gold
or wheat. Farmers, or maybe gamblers,

were shoveling coal into the firebox
along with Indians and wolves. In the pilot house
preachers and bankers, lawyers and swindlers
platted the prairies, forests and swamps.

Struggling to wake up, I turned on a lamp
and ghosts of salmon smolts poured out.
The light rattled like coins. The hammering kept on,
but it wasn't in the river now, it was in my head.

I went to the sink and opened the tap. Clear water
spilled out, cool and fresh. It had all been a dream.
The river was leaping with fish, muscled with joy.
I was so pleased. I was innocent. I was still asleep.

Tap Water

On a hot day that first cold sip
is electric. The tongue wakes up
and wags its tail.

Now nose and hindbrain
detect an aftertaste:
chlorine, alum,

and the cerebellum interjects
sad history,
river sewer.

Another swallow, a pause
to smack the lips, watch bubbles
rise like thoughts . . . and burst!

Now comes affluence—
rhythmically glugging down
the entire glass,

glottis pulsing in the tide wash happy as a kelp,
throat constricting and releasing
in continuous little orgasms . . .

Ah, tap water! Mountain snow,
river, ocean, sky. And back
to the heat of the day.

Toil

I was digging a trench to plant spuds in,
starting to really sweat,
glasses fogging, knees clicking,
when the last of a winter flu bug gripped my chest.
I leaned on my spade,
wheezing...

What will happen
when I can't dig anymore?
What happens
to a word
when we quit using it?
What glue factory do we send words to
when they stumble and can't pull the plow?

I want to rescue that old word *toil*,
bring it home
and put it to pasture in my backyard.
I want to rub noses with it
and brush the burrs from its tail.

So I do. I bring it home. Look, I say,
help me toil in the garden.
We'll grow cabbages
and images, turnips and opinions.
We'll write old poems
with lines like—

He toiled in fields
the color of his skin.
                    Or,
The toil she knew
told in her hands.

Hold still, I say,
to that half starved word.
I'm strong as a mule.
I'll pull you.

Solar Gain

Just breathing
on a January afternoon

with the winter sun
streaming through the window

kindling my cheeks.
I'm being

efficient.
Eyes closed,

mind on idle,
I'm thermal mass

and not much more.
I doze and dream

and store up warmth,
generating some mild

photovoltaics
in the mind—

feeling as the maple tree
must feel

on the verge
of leafing out.

When the Pipes Freeze on Christmas Eve
I Crawl Under the House with My Wife's Hair
Dryer and a Trouble Light

Some unwelcome guest—
a raccoon, maybe, or a cat—
has shredded the insulation from the copper pipe
where it rises out of the ground.

I crawl to the far corner,
prop myself on one elbow, aim the hair dryer
and look around

at all the little packages
dangling from the floor joists
wrapped in gobs of dust and moldering cobwebs—gifts
from Santa's doppelganger,
the evil twin brother who lives at the *other* pole.

Gifts of husks
and vacancies, of loss and
desolation. Maybe the gift of
empty space
every death makes for the rest of us.

By the time the pipe thaws
and the water gurgles back to life,
I have remembered many such gifts, and I'm ready
for a hot shower
and a little celebrating.

Sacred Space

Lying on my back
in the crawl space under the house,
holding a length of two-inch ABS drain line
snug in the fitting while the glue dries,

I think of other such dim,
constricted places: the stinking
refrigerator I nearly suffocated in once
playing hide and seek,

the privet hedge I crawled under
whenever my father got drunk,

and that cave in Tibet
where Milarepa lived,
subsisting on nettles
until his body turned a lovely shade of blue.

Five Poems for Kapa

1. Her Passion

We usually keep Christmas
pretty minimal—a handmade card,
a full-body massage.
Always a pair of earrings for her, and for me
my favorite socks. But this year

she asks, turning shy
as we hike the forested path up Dimple Hill,
if I'll get her something special:
rocks.

Specifically, she'd like
a pallet of quartzite sandstone or Camas basalt—
two or three tons of big, flat slabs
to frame a garden bed
beside the path to the front door.

I love
how middle age has made her
desirous,
how her passion
has become so discrete. I ask,

How about a flannel nightie
to go along with that?
Or a weekend at the beach?
Thanks, she says, squeezing my hand,
just the rocks.

2. Walking Pneumonia

Coughing and wheezing,
we're out for a walk, pausing often to
gawk at a crocus, to hack and spit.

We'd be fools to believe
the worst is behind us, to let these
red-eyed vireos, ferreting

insects from the maple, infect us
with their feverish appetites,
their vehement happiness.

When a skein of geese honks over,
you squeeze my hand and gasp
with pleasure. We are

fools. We do believe. We lean
our heads together
and watch a pair of vultures circle above us,

soaring higher and higher
until they wheel
clean out of sight.

3. The Meadow

Wild grasses up to our waists,
we plunge through the meadow,

running our fingers over the seed heads,
tossing handfuls of grain in each other's hair.

I'll bet we could eat these, you say,
chewing a stem, pulling me down.

4. Aspens and Vandals

West Side

Firs, alders, and maples
grow thick and intermingled
here in the Valley, and the undergrowth
of snowberry and Indian plum gets all snarled up
with Himalayan blackberry. Throw in

the rank entanglements
of e-mail, job obligations, family
snits and it gets a little
claustrophobic.

I need a road trip, a couple of nights
camping solo on the east side, a quick jaunt into
low-down loneliness
to remind me how much I miss your touch
when I go without it for a while.

East Side

Beyond Madras
every juniper has bare ground around it,
the space I've been craving.
Through the Ochocos
the highway flickers between
overgrown lodgepoles, skinny
and dying, but down
a nameless dirt road I find a grove
of big ponderosas
and at the far end of a meadowy swale

a dozen aspens rustle and sway
in the evening breeze.

Remember our honeymoon
in the Strawberries twenty years ago,
camped in a grove of aspens
that sugared the air and turned every breeze
to a whispering voice? That's where
we punctured our air mattress
making love without checking for twigs.

Now, at dusk, missing you,
I walk among the aspens
touching their trunks, breathing their scent,
and trying to picture the lovers,
deer hunters, and beer guzzling vandals
who have carved their initials into all these trees.

Alone in the mountains, beyond
cell phone reception, lonelier
than I set out to be, I fall back
on old technology and an outmoded brand
of sentiment—
                    with evening coming on,
in the bark of a slender young aspen
I carve our initials inside a fresh heart.

5. Little River

Remember the time we made love
on the banks of the Calapooia, our trashy

local river, then flipped the canoe
in a little riffle downstream?

Such are the virtues
I adore in you—

that you don't need big rapids
or exotic scenery

to risk drowning
or ecstasy.

IV.

Centipede

When I'm feeling old—
when my knees creak, or my eyes water
in the mildest breeze,
or I get winded from a short flight
of stairs—

I think of the centipede
who has not changed in habit, appearance,
or attitude
for three million years.

I should walk more
articulately. I should keep
closer to the Earth. I could even
shimmy like the centipede,

or pretend my legs
were a hundred oars. Yes,
I can almost see
the farther shore.
All together now, boys,
pull.

Unnamed

I'm sitting at the picnic table
trying to write
while batting away flies—

horseflies, houseflies, sawflies, bottle flies . . .

How many flies
does this planet need!

Well, enough
to carry the news
between flowers, I suppose,

and a few to impregnate
the road killed doe.

One broken one
expiring in the duff
after biting my neck

and one metallic green
futuristic model, all bristles and eyeballs,
standing nonchalantly on my notebook

rubbing its eyes in disbelief
at the naiveté of a certain biped
who shall go unnamed.

Puddling

A big white butterfly
with reddish eyes
      on its hind wings

is lapping up minerals
from a damp spot beside a puddle
      in the high Wallowas.

I believe it would treasure
      polysyllabic words
and challenging concepts—like *spermatophore*
or *nuptial gift*—
      if it were me

because
      I can just taste
those pungent salts
at the edge of the puddle

and I know when it's time
to rise up flapping
    and glide
down that long field of yarrow.

Pillillooeet

Studying ways
to germinate in place

I watch Pillillooeet
scamper the canopy
of a big old Sitka spruce
outside the cabin
on Cascade Head
at the Oregon Coast.

Listening as spruce cones
thump the roof
I vow
to be diligent
and to scatter seeds freely.

"The Douglas Squirrel surpasses
every other species in force of character.
A King's River Indian told me
they call him 'Pillillooeet,' which,
rapidly pronounced . . . is not unlike
the lusty exclamation he utters when excited."

When I step outside
Pillillooeet

scrambles fast
face down
down the tree

and shouts his name
like a manic
squeaky toy.

The many neat mounds
of spruce cone scales
he leaves on stairs and stumps

might be artistic
debris or eloquent
industry

but what he's after
is the seed
same as me.

Grass

Walking down toward the meadow
I catch a spider web
      smack in the face

and I think of those
      coyotes
that stalked my tent last night
howling close by. Were they
      trying to mess with me?
        Barbaric
yawping, it sounded like. . . .

So I look under my boot soles
      for old Walt
but the grass appears to be just
green-bladed manufactories

cranking out carbohydrates
      that ungulates
        like to eat.

But then, kneeling down and
      squinting obliquely
toward the rising sun, I see that grass indeed
      is the green pelt
        of a powerful beast

and I feel myself plunging into the day
    as if perched on a whale.

Into the Wind

Alley cats of the sand.
Beach bum birds.
Avian spawn of garbage dumps.
Those pretty white spatters all over the parking lot
are their artwork.

The only good thing I can say for seagulls is this:
those week old donuts
the bag lady is throwing out for them,
they deserve.

On the other hand, just yesterday
I was out on the jetty
when a seagull hurtled past me
speeding *into the wind.*

How does it do that?
Does it find some seam in the air
where everything is still?
Does it do some kind of jiujitsu
that rolls the wind around its wings
and pushes it from behind?

Whatever it does,
I want some. Seems like my life
is getting down to old donuts
and shit on the sidewalk.
I have no idea where I'm going,
but if I could just cut through this headwind
I could get there faster.

Dragonflies

At first they seem paramilitary,
rattling above the lakeshore reeds,
conning the shore for anything edible,
some kind of carnivorous machine.

But the longer I drift
in this borrowed boat
at the shallow margins of a mountain lake,
the more inquisitive they become, landing on the oar
beside my grub-white fingers,
sniffing my intentions,
studying me
with their finely tooled eyes.

Now one clatters up
and circles my head
as if testing my compass.
And now it hovers in the air
before my third eye—a hypnotist
willing me to open my soul.

I resist.
It's almost dusk. My friends
have kindled a fire back at camp. I ply the oars.

But the dragonflies
are mating now, clacking their wings,
and crashing together like
crazy little gods,
like furious forgiveness,

like a man and a woman,
young, scared,
screwing themselves up to strange heights, loving
and hurting each other
one last night
before he gets shipped off to the war.

The Terravores

I'm going to miss them,
those lumbering yellow road graders,
bulldozers, and belly scrapers
grazing at the edge of town.

When the gas is gone, I'll miss
watching the little boys
point and squeal with excitement
as the big machines unerringly
peel the face from another wheat field.

Most of all, I'll miss
their awful placidity
at night, bedded down
in the moonshade of scorched oaks
like perfect beasts.

Winter Solstice at Road's End

Tide's out. Setting sun
gleams red on the breakers.
Those orange lights
on the far horizon
must be fishing boats.

Last week a crabber capsized
on the bar at Coos Bay,
the skipper drowned. The coho run
is supposed to be up this year,
sockeyes down.

The wide beach is nearly empty,
just a pair of staggering lovers
and an old woman in rubber boots.
I watch a rivulet
spill from its pipe in the bluff,

fan out across the sand
in shifting channels
like a prostrate tree
or the nerves in a body,
a mock river flowing down to the shore.

Where the murky drainwater
merges with the surf,
a few seagulls wait,
hoping to feed
on whatever little life the trickle bears.

Not an Omen

We're watching a lurid sunset
turn blood-red, bruise-blue,
the roiling cumulonimbus
tinted with oxides of nitrogen and sulfur
courtesy of a forest fire over by Sisters.

Knowing the compromised origin
of this breathtaking spectacle
muddles our pleasure with vague unease,
though you insist beauty is often messed up
with smoke, fire, and fumes.

So we probably shouldn't read too much
into the scrub jay's startled exclamation,
or take the abrupt departure of several dozen robins
as an omen of anything but nature's
inscrutable coming and going.

But now the wind picks up
and a fierce gust rips a branch
from the big-leaf maple.
Lights snuff out on the horizon.
Clouds pour in from the coast.

Out of the west comes an awful cawing,
then a scripture of crows scribbles the sky
hurtled along on a pelt of rain,
their cries falling like scraps of burnt text
on our tenuous peace of mind.

Coda: Turkey Vulture Talking

It's probably true I think too much,
sitting all night in my dead tree.
But I'm a changed bird come sunrise—
Mr. Transformer, Mr. Capability.

So maybe I can't fly worth a hoot,
drunk all the time on old meat.
I'm honest. Reliable.
I'll get to the job if I have to walk.

Oh, just a wobbly old buzzard,
not good for much. Cogitating,
regurgitating, ferrying souls
across that final river,
getting sadder and uglier . . .

Is it worth it?
Look at me—

I've still got my appetite.

Notes

"White Galaxy" is in memory of John Thomas (Tom) Goodrich, December 6, 1911–June 1, 1978. His one published novel, *Cotton Cavalier* (Farrar and Rinehart, 1932) was widely praised and reviewed.

"A Shrine" is in memory of Franz Dolp.

"Black Bug" and "Fern in the Bumper" are in memory of the superb Oregon poet Richard Dankleff (1925–2010).

"At Rattlesnake Pass" is for James Nash.

"The Piano Tuner" is for (and, in part, by) Anita Sullivan.

"Rocks for Seeds" is for Linda and John Hussa.

"Pillillooeet": The quote is from John Muir, *The Mountains of California*, where Muir dedicates an entire chapter to the Douglas Squirrel, *Tamiasciurus douglasii*.

"Puddling" is for Robert Michael Pyle. In reply to my query, Bob told me the butterfly in question was most likely *Parnassius smintheus*.

Acknowledgments

Gratitude to the editors of the following journals, in which many of these poems, sometimes under different titles or in different forms, first appeared:

Cloudbank: "Sacred Space"; *High Desert Journal*: "A Distant Relative," "Grinding Wheel," "Origins"; *Oregon Humanities*: "Rocks for Seeds"; *Willow Springs*: "Coda: Turkey Vulture Talking"; *Wilderness*: "Solar Gain"; and *Windfall*: "Burdock," "Black Bug," "Dragonflies," "Terravores."

"Filament" and "The Uber-Rich Step Up" were first published as broadsides by Tangram Press.

"Aspens and Vandals" was composed for the serial poem sequence, "These Mountains That Separate Us," a collaboration among poets from the east and west sides of the Cascades, initiated by Jack E. Lorts and published in book form by Traprock Books, 2012.

"Daoist Out of Kansas" will appear in the anthology, *A Ritual to Read Together: Poems in Conversation with William Stafford*, edited by Becca J. R. Lachman, Woodley Press, 2013.

"Ghost River" appeared in the anthology, *What the River Brings*, edited by Kathryn Ridall, Fae Press, 2012.

"Tap Water" is included as part of an art work installation, *The Willamette*, by William Shumway at the Corvallis-Benton County Public Library.

"Burdock" was reprinted in *Ecology of Weeds and Invasive Plants: Relationship to Agriculture and Natural Resource Management*, by Steven R. Radosevich, Jodie S. Holt, Claudio M. Ghersa, published by John Wiley & Sons, 2007.

The following poems were written at the Sitka Center for Art and Ecology, and offered as contributions to the Sitka Reflections Project: "Pillillooeet," "Into the Wind," "Winter Solstice at Road's End."

The following poems were originally published in a chapbook, *In the Chesnim Country* (Fishtrap, 2010), which was the product of my month as the Fishtrap/Werner Writer-in-Residence in Wallowa County: "The Nature of Fear," "Puddling," "Grinding Wheel," "Origins," "Wallowa County Weather," "Government Work," "Morning Song at Billy Meadows," "At Rattlesnake Pass," "Grass," "Unnamed," and "Un-making the Sky."

Gratitude to the generous and perspicacious writers who commented on the manuscript: Rick Borsten, Gregg Kleiner, Kathleen Dean Moore, Clemens Starck.

The interior text and display type as well as the back cover text were set in Adobe Jenson, a faithful electronic version of the 1470 roman face of Nicolas Jenson. Jenson was a Frenchman employed as the mintmaster at Tours. Legend has it that he was sent to Mainz in 1458 by Charles VII to learn the new art of printing in the shop of Gutenberg, and import it to France. But he never returned, appearing in Venice in 1468; there his first roman types appeared, in his edition of Eusebius. He moved to Rome at the invitation of Pope Sixtus IV, where he died in 1480.

Type historian Daniel Berkeley Updike praises the Jenson Roman for "its readability, its mellowness of form, and the evenness of color in mass." Updike concludes, "Jenson's roman types have been the accepted models for roman letters ever since he made them, and, repeatedly copied in our own day, have never been equalled."

The typeface used for the front cover text is Arno. Named after the Florentine river which runs through the heart of the Italian Renaissance, Arno draws on the warmth and readability of early humanist typefaces of the 15th and 16th centuries. While inspired by the past, Arno is distinctly contemporary in both appearance and function. Designed by Adobe Principal Designer Robert Slimbach, Arno is a meticulously crafted face in the tradition of early Venetian and Aldine book typefaces. Embodying themes Slimbach has explored in typefaces such as Minion and Brioso, Arno represents a distillation of his design ideals and a refinement of his craft.

Silverfish Review Press is committed to preserving ancient forests and natural resources. We elected to print *A Scripture of Crows* on 30% post consumer recycled paper, processed chlorine free. As a result, for this printing, we have saved: 1 tree (40' tall and 6-8" diameter), 499 gallons of water, 293 kilowatt hours of electricity, 64 pounds of solid waste, and 120 pounds of greenhouse gases. Thomson-Shore, Inc. is a member of Green Press Initiative, a nonprofit program dedicated to supporting authors, publishers, and suppliers in their efforts to reduce their use of fiber obtained from endangered forests. For more information, visit www.greenpressinitiative.org.

Cover design by Valerie Brewster, Scribe Typography.
Text design by Rodger Moody and Connie Kudura, ProtoType.
Printed on acid-free papers and bound by Thomson-Shore, Inc.